Self Explorations

BY CORINA STUPU THOMAS

PUBLISHED IN 2020 BY
KDPSELECT

@CORINA STUPU THOMAS

COVER DESIGN BY CORINA
STUPU THOMAS

ISBN - 9798651408542

Self Explorations

Modern lifestyles have the effect of denying us the chance of a deeper connection with our inner self. We are constantly distracted by TV or the latest pop-up message, or by the latest series on the latest streaming service that "everybody" raves about, or the new clothes we see somewhere, or the 2 for 1 offers attracting us to buy even more ....with little thought, or the newest superfood we rush to find, ever so hopeful it will make us healthier in weeks or slimmer. We are ... always watching, watching, watching..... something outside of us.

Yet... in spite of all of these outward experiences... we too often find ourselves confused, distraught, tired. And so many times we end up with a sense of longing, for a miraculous something that will add more meaning and joy to our lives.
×××××

"Self Explorations" is a practical workbook aiming to help you to understand yourself better ......with a pen in your hand, to write down what comes into your mind...and in doing so, to establish a stronger sense of SELF.
×××××

The world has been through lockdown, an unprecedented moment in modern history, when it did not matter who you were, what social class you belonged to, whether you were part of a big family or a tiny one, whatever nationality you were, rich or poor ... .we all had to obey other people's rules, to stay indoors, doing the best we could to keep ourselves sane, fully occupied and mentally balanced.

For the first time in a long time we had to discover our inner resources, to survive the rainbow of emotions that nobody is immune to ... from joy to desperation, from hopelessness to empowerment .... we went through all of that and more. It was a time to get to know our nearest and dearest better, it was also a time to discover our coping mechanisms, to discover what really mattered to us, to understand what we want or do not want or need anymore.

"We don't develop courage by being happy every day.
We develop it by surviving difficult times and challenging adversity"
– Barbara de Angelis

Purpose of the book

Consider this workbook to be an invitation to an inner archeological expedition behind the layers of pain, disappointment, fear, achievements and values ....and in doing so....to reconnect with your true self ....and:

@ re-acquaint yourself with your real values;
@ remind yourself of your achievements;
@ better understand your reasoning,
@ so that you can better express your needs,
@ build your self-confidence,
@ create a deeper connection between images and words.
@ simplify your life and be more fulfilled,
@ relax and enter a meditative state through writing, creative colouring, daily gratitude and collage making

"My true identity goes beyond the outer roles I play ... there is an authentic "I" within ...a divine spark within the soul. " – Sue Monk Kidd

Sometimes, we need to be reminded that in order to arrive at this moment in our lives, we've survived many upsetting, challenging, disturbing times. And that ... in spite of all this, we are still here, still standing, with a wealth of experience behind us, with many moments deserving to be acknowledged and celebrated.

The workbook has four themes

Theme 1 –   Know yourself
Theme 2 a – Daily gratitude practice – 4 weeks
Theme 2b – Creative colouring practice
Theme 3 –   Self expression through collage practice
Theme 4 –   Who I am – choosing 3 out of 50

What to do, where to start

Simply open the workbook and start wherever you land, wherever you want. There are no rules. Simply listen to your intuition. Remember that you can come back to the same question again and again, that you don't need to finish any task in one go. Take you time! Be supportive of yourself – always.

Theme 1 KNOW YOURSELF

Prompts will invite you to explore various topics. But, before you start each prompt, centre yourself – take a few deep breaths, put on your favourite music or sit somewhere in nature or, if you are at home, light a candle, bring next to you an object that you have a special connection with. Create a cosy space around you ... if that is not always possible .. imagine it. Imagination is a very powerful tool!

In answering the invitation of the prompt one of the most important things is to allow your words or images to arrive on the page without any censorship, writing in any way you want ... from right to left, left to right, you can turn the workbook upside down ... give yourself permission to break rules .. because there are no rules here – and listen to your needs.

When you complete one of the prompts (it might take you a day or weeks) look back at the pages you have completed and choose three findings that were the most important or relevant to you at that moment in time. Record them at the end of the workbook in the spare pages provided for you. called " 3 out of 50". Think about how those three special findings helped you at that time. Be prepared to be amazed! .

Theme 2a   DAILY GRATITUDE PRACTICE

"Gratitude unlocks the fulness of life. It can turn a meal into a feast, a house into a home, a stranger into a friend." – Melody Beattie

So many times life overwhelms us and even if we've had quite a good day, just one little thing can upset us, and hours later, we still dwell on that negative thing. It is human nature. By starting a gratitude journal you will interrupt the chain of negative thoughts and start noticing more of the good things that happened in your life.

X x X X x x

Make a commitment to start a four week gratitude practice. If you don't fill in a page for a particular day ... don't worry .. simply come back to the page later and carry on – but remember to write the date on top of the page. .

You might find it hard to start a gratitude practice at the beginning, words might not want to come onto the page easily - but with daily practice and perseverance, words will soon flow, you will have opened the door to positive thoughts. Just start! Start now!

X x X X x x

What gratitude practice does is change your perception of the state of balance in your life and the world around you. It will make your life feel brighter! Gratitude is like a muscle .. it thrives with practice and repetition. So, remember to say an inner THANK YOU when you finish your daily practice. It is a THANK YOU...to yourself! And give yourself a warm, loving hug! Say to yourself! I AM A SAFE! ALL IS WELL!

"When we focus on our gratitude, the tide of disappointment goes out and the tide of love rushes in. " – Kristin Armstrong

Theme 2b CREATIVE COLOURING

When I say that colouring-in helps to reduce anxiety and stress, that it is a form of creative meditation, that it improves sleep and helps one focus, that it helps replace the negative patterns of thinking with positive ones, I am speaking from my personal experience and I know it to be true.

It really does not matter what materials you have at home ... you can start with whatever you have ... colourful pens, juicy pens, watercolours, acrylics, oil pastels, watercolour pencils .. and you can combine them as well if you want. The practice of creative colouring tells a lot about us. Do we seek perfection and put ourselves under pressure or can we relax easily allowing us to simply enjoy the moment?

Theme 3 SELF EXPRESSION THROUGH COLLAGE PRACTICE

Expressing our feelings and thoughts through images allows us to go to a deeper place in our minds, helping us to tell and re-tell stories deeply buried within us, stories that are sometimes hard to express through just words.

Be prepared to be amazed by the images you choose, by the way you combine them on the paper, remembering always that the visual language you are embracing is the oldest language of all times, yes it is.

Visual languages existed before human beings could capture the thoughts in a written form. Self expression through images takes the oldest form of language and blends with the youngest – to produce images that truly bring meaning.

WHAT YOU THINK YOU BECOME WHAT YOU FEEL YOU ATTRACT WHAT YOU IMAGINE YOU CREATE

*Our actions and decisions today will shape
the way we will be living in the future.*

Theme 1 - Know yourself!

Left, right and centre we are encouraged by various gurus of the day to … be ourselves. In a society where we are encouraged, and most of the times scared into conforming and following whatever others want us to believe and do, it is harder and harder to actually express who we are … our essence, our core values, what we stand for, what makes us unique, what we like, what makes us … US!

Repetition - transforming recollections and random thoughts into the authentic YOU

It was Aristotle, the Ancient Greece philosopher, who is reported to have commented: "It is frequent repetition that produces a natural tendency…. how knowledge can become second nature". Observers of habits have also noted that with practice, and practice, and practice, a person does not need to think consciously about something ……because it has become embedded in the subconscious.

Throughout my workbook I provide you with prompts that invite you to explore many subjects – and later I ask you to choose just a few of them and explore these even more – what it will do is help you form a clearer sense of the authentic YOU and give you a clearer idea as to how to move forward stronger and with more clarity!

ENJOY THE JOURNEY!

50 things I love about my life

....

....

....

....

....

....

....

....

....

I AM UNIQUE

50 things I love about my life

....

....

....

....

....

....

....

....

....

....

I AM COMPETENT

50 things I love about my life

....

....

....

....

....

....

....

....

....

I AM MOTIVATED

50 ways to describe myself

....

....

....

....

....

....

....

....

....

....

I AM OK

50 ways to describe myself

....

....

....

....

....

....

....

....

....

I AM CURIOUS

50 ways to describe myself

....

....

....

....

....

....

....

....

....

....

I AM AMBITIOUS

It is not beauty that endears, it's love that makes us see beauty.

LEO TOLSTOY

50 life principles you live by

··

··

··

··

··

··

··

··

··

··

I AM ADVENTUROUS

50 life principles you live by

....

....

....

....

....

....

....

....

....

....

I AM LOVABLE

50 life principles you live by

....

....

....

....

....

....

....

....

....

....

I AM JOYFUL

50 childhood memories

. . . .

. . . .

. . . .

. . . .

. . . .

. . . .

. . . .

. . . .

. . . .

. . . .

I AM RESPONSIBLE

50 childhood memories

....

....

....

....

....

....

....

....

....

....

I AM COURAGEOUS

50 childhood memories

....

....

....

....

....

....

....

....

....

....

I AM CREATIVE

50 things I need to forgive abOut myself

....

....

....

....

....

....

....

....

....

....

I AM BRAVE

50 things I need to
forgive abOut myself

....

....

....

....

....

....

....

....

....

....

I AM DELICATE

50 things I need to forgive abOut myself

···

···

···

···

···

···

···

···

···

···

I AM HONEST

50 skills I have

....

....

....

....

....

....

....

....

....

....

I AM ME

50 skills I have

....

....

....

....

....

....

....

....

....

....

I AM PASSIONATE

50 skills I have

....

....

....

....

....

....

....

....

....

....

I AM MINDFUL

live
laugh
love

50 ways to show myself kindness

....

....

....

....

....

....

....

....

....

I AM KIND

50 ways to show myself kindness

....

....

....

....

....

....

....

....

....

....

> **I AM OPEN TO NEW ADVENTURES**

50 ways to show myself kindness

....

....

....

....

....

....

....

....

....

....

I AM OPEN TO NEW
FRIENDSHIPS

50 questions you would like to be asked by a friend or counselor

....

....

....

....

....

....

....

....

....

I AM WORTHY

50 questions you would like to be asked by a friend or counselor

....

....

....

....

....

....

....

....

....

....

I AM COMPASSIONATE

50 questions you would like to be asked by a friend or counselor

··
··
··
··
··
··
··
··
··
··

I AM GRATEFUL

50 questions you would like to ask the divine/Mother Earth

....

....

....

....

....

....

....

....

....

....

I AM PATIENT

50 questions you would like to ask the divine/Mother Earth

....

....

....

....

....

....

....

....

....

I AM ENOUGH

50 questions you would like to ask the divine/Mother Earth

....

....

....

....

....

....

....

....

....

....

I AM INSPIRED

50 jobs you would love to have even if for 1 day

....

....

....

....

....

....

....

....

....

I AM RESOURCEFUL

50 jobs you would love
to have even if for 1 day

....

....

....

....

....

....

....

....

....

....

I AM FUNNY

50 jobs you would love to have even if for 1 day

··

··

··

··

··

··

··

··

··

··

I AM PRESENT

50 things you've learned about yourself in lockdown

....

....

....

....

....

....

....

....

....

....

I AM RESILIENT

50 things you've learned about yourself in lockdown

....

....

....

....

....

....

....

....

....

I AM PROUD

50 things you've learned about yourself in lockdown

....

....

....

....

....

....

....

....

....

....

I AM HERE

Show yourself

KINDNESS

GENEROSITY

ACCEPTANCE

50 things you would like to see, learn, experience

· ·

· ·

· ·

· ·

· ·

· ·

· ·

· ·

· ·

· ·

I AM LOVED

50 things you would like to see, learn, experience

....

....

....

....

....

....

....

....

....

I AM FRIENDLY

50 things you would like to see, learn, experience

· ·

· ·

· ·

· ·

· ·

· ·

· ·

· ·

· ·

· ·

I AM BEAUTIFUL

50 things you've done that you are proud of

....

....

....

....

....

....

....

....

....

....

I AM WHO I AM

50 things you've done that you are proud of

....

....

....

....

....

....

....

....

....

....

I AM AUTHENTIC

50 things you've done that you are proud of

....

....

....

....

....

....

....

....

....

I AM HAPPY TO BE ME

50 ways to simplify
your life

....

....

....

....

....

....

....

....

....

....

I AM CONFIDENT

50 ways to simplify
your life

··

··

··

··

··

··

··

··

··

··

I AM GENEROUS

50 ways to simplify
your life

. . . .

. . . .

. . . .

. . . .

. . . .

. . . .

. . . .

. . . .

. . . .

. . . .

I AM OPTIMISTIC

50 kinds of help that you need now

....

....

....

....

....

....

....

....

....

I AM AN EXPLORER

50 kinds of help that you need now

....

....

....

....

....

....

....

....

....

....

> **EMBRACE THE DAY**

50 kinds of help that you need now

....

....

....

....

....

....

....

....

....

....

EVERYTHING IS POSSIBLE

All you need is love.
But a little chocolate
now and then
doesn't hurt.

CHARLES M. SCHULZ

I always wanted to

For the next 7 days pick something that you wanted to have a go at but postponed because life got in the way – and promise yourself you will have a go at it. It does not have to be something that requires a lot of time. Start with baby steps and do that particular something for a few minutes a day. Describe your feelings, circumstances and daily progress

Day

I always wanted to

Day ②

Day ③

I always wanted to

Day

Day 5

I always wanted to

Day 6

Day 7

Now that your eyes are open, make the sun jealous with your burning passion to start the day.

MALAK EL HALABI

DO SOMETHING TODAY THAT YOUR FUTURE SELF WILL THANK YOU FOR.

How do you want to feel?
Express in words!

Pick up your pen and start writing about how you would you like to feel. Write a string of words without any connection with each other or write it in the form of a short story. Just write! Allow your intuition to be in the driving seat. Write the words on two separate days!

How do you want to feel?
Express in words!

How do you want to feel?
Express in words!

How do you want to feel?
Create a collage!

Pick up a couple of magazines and a tube of glue. No scissors needed at all. Look at the question, browse through the magazines and begin to paste in the images that speak to you. When you finish, take a step back and look at the images. What do they say to you? Is there anything that surprises you? Do this on two separate days!

How do you want to feel?
Create a collage!

How do you want to feel?
Create a collage!

What do you need in order to be fulfilled? Express in words!

We rush everywhere! Many times we eat without noticing what we eat, we drive without noticing the environment, we meet people and at the end of the day we forget who they were. Our minds operate on auto pilot. We watch TV and are bombarded by adversiting, advertising making us want various things without much thinking. We chase other people's dreams. Stop for a few minutes and think for yourself. Think and write .. What do you really need in order to be fulfilled? Write on two separate days!

What do you need in order to be fulfilled? Express in words!

What do you need in order to be fulfilled? Express in words!

What do you need in order to be fulfilled? Create a collage?

Pick up a couple of magazines and a tube of glue. Look at the question and see what images connect with you, what images answer to the question above. Use your gut feeling. It does not need to make sense ... simply follow your intuition. Paste these images into this workbook. At the end, take some time and look to see if there is anything that surprises you. What story can you tell based on the images? Do this on two separate days!

What do you need in order to be fulfilled? Create a collage?

What do you need in order to be fulfilled? Create a collage!

Who inspires you and why?
Express in words!

Role models are extremely important in our lives. One person can change your life forever through their emotional support, advice, guidance, example of a life well lived, belief in you and your mission in this world! Think about one person who is your role model and write about him or her. How did you meet? How did he or she influence your life and why. What would you tell her or him if he or she were to stand in front of you. Pick up your pen and write for 20 minutes. ,

Who inspires you and why?
Express in words!

Who inspires you and why?
Express in words!

Fake news in the media you become aware of!

Modern life means that we are bombarded by news. News from our friends, from the on line platforms, from the traditional media, from our families. More than ever before fake news is being used to ignite various reactions in us all, change our perceptions about reality, events, stories. Research 3 fake news stories and write about the way they impacted on you. What can you do to help yourself to identify which news is fake.

Fake news 1

Fake news in the media you became aware of?

Fake news 2

Fake news in the media you became aware of?

Fake news 3

Fake "information" you believe about yourself

What are the 3 things you keep believing about yourself although you have no proof it is true and yet it makes you live your life with the hand break on. Think about your limiting beliefs first of all. Those limiting beliefs are very much like ... the fake news. How would your life look if you dismiss those limiting beliefs? How would you feel? What would you do? Simply write ....

Fake information ①

Fake "information" you believe about yourself

Fake information 2

Fake "information" you believe about yourself

Fake information 3

DREAM BIG,
WORK HARD,
- MAKE IT -
happen.

THEME 2

DAILY GRATITUDE- 4 WEEKS

For the next month scribble down anything positive that has happened during the day, anything you are thankful for no matter how big or small. You know and I know that each day is different. This practice will help you to be more in the here and now and also to be more observant of our realities and to be less spaced out, living in the past or future. Observe how your daily writings will deepen your connection with your life and help you clarify some of the issues that bother you. Remember to be spontaneous!

Enjoy the creative colouring pages peppered among the gratitude practice!

"Only in spontaneity can we be who we truly are" - John Mclaughlin

I AM GRATEFUL

Describe your day in 1 word or symbol

I AM GRATEFUL

Describe your day in 1 word or symbol

I AM GRATEFUL

Describe your day in 1 word or symbol

I AM GRATEFUL

Describe your day in 1 word or symbol

I AM GRATEFUL

Describe your day in 1 word or symbol

I AM GRATEFUL

Describe your day in 1 word or symbol

I AM GRATEFUL

Describe your day in 1 word or symbol

I AM GRATEFUL

Describe your day in 1 word or symbol

I AM GRATEFUL

Describe your day in 1 word or symbol

I AM GRATEFUL

Describe your day in 1 word or symbol

I AM GRATEFUL

Describe your day in 1 word or symbol

I AM GRATEFUL

Describe your day in 1 word or symbol

I AM GRATEFUL

Describe your day in 1 word or symbol

I AM GRATEFUL

Describe your day in 1 word or symbol

I AM GRATEFUL

Describe your day in 1 word or symbol

I AM GRATEFUL

Describe your day in 1 word or symbol

I AM GRATEFUL

Describe your day in 1 word or symbol

I AM GRATEFUL

Describe your day in 1 word or symbol

I AM GRATEFUL

Describe your day in 1 word or symbol

I AM GRATEFUL

Describe your day in 1 word or symbol

I AM GRATEFUL

Describe your day in 1 word or symbol

I AM GRATEFUL

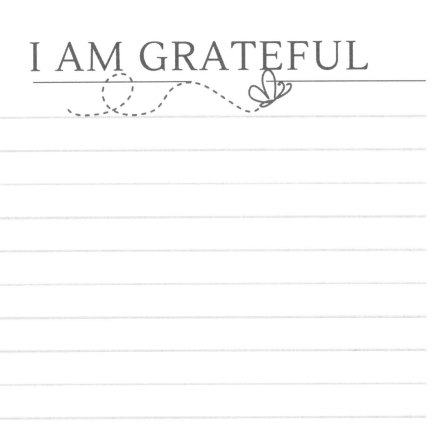

Describe your day in 1 word or symbol

I AM GRATEFUL

Describe your day in 1 word or symbol

I AM GRATEFUL

Describe your day in 1 word or symbol

I AM GRATEFUL

Describe your day in 1 word or symbol

I AM GRATEFUL

Describe your day in 1 word or symbol

I AM GRATEFUL

Describe your day in 1 word or symbol

I AM GRATEFUL

Describe your day in 1 word or symbol

BE YOURSELF AND LIVE LIFE YOUR WAY. IT'S THE KEY TO YOUR HAPPINESS!

Theme 3 COLLAGE PRACTICE

Sometimes, an image speaks louder than just words. Sometimes it is easier to express what we feel through the visual language. This is an invitation to do exactly that ... use words AND images from magazines, newspapers, your own photos and create collages that speak to you using the promts suggested or simply choose your own subject. .

COLLAGE practice
Self love

X x X X X x

Think about the word self love! We use it quite a lot but .... what does it actually mean to you? Create a collage containing images and words from magazines that speak to you and represent self love! Get a stack of magazines, newspapers, glue and remember to allow your intution to be in the driver's seat!

COLLAGE practice
Self love
✗ ✗ ✗ ✗ ✗ ✗

COLLAGE practice
Together we are strong
X x X X X x

Together we are strong. Create a collage containing images that speak
to you and represent the subject! Get a stack of magazines, newspapers,
glue and remember to allow the intution to be in the driver's seat!

COLLAGE practice
Together we are strong

COLLAGE practice
Nature heals me

Nature heals me! Create a collage containing images that speak to you
and represent the subject! Get a stack of magazines, newspapers, glue
 and remember to allow the intution to be in the driver's seat!

COLLAGE practice
Nature heals me
X x X X X x

COLLAGE practice
The sea

The sea is always a source of peace and healing. Create a collage containing images that speak to you and represent the subject! Get a stack of magazines, newspapers, glue and remember to allow the intution to be in the driver's seat!

COLLAGE practice
The sea
✕ ✕ ✕ ✕ ✕ ✕

YOU HAVE

TO BE KIND

TO YOURSELF

I AM STILL HERE

Describe 50 challenging moments in your life .... write them down and next to each of them write ..... in spite of all of that ... I am still here!

I AM STILL HERE

I AM STILL HERE

WHO I AM – 3 out of 50

In this last section, write again, yes, 3 of your entries in EACH of the headings in theme 1 – KNOW YOURSELF that mean the most to you. And, choose and write 10 out all of your GRATITUDE PRACTICE entries in theme 2, that mean the most to you.

Then sit back, reflect and congratulate yourself. What you have done is piece together, create a collage of all that you really are, the totality of all that you value and all that you aspire to be.

GOOD ON YOU!

WHO I AM – 3 out of 50

WHO I AM – 3 out of 50

WHO AM I – 3 out of 50

WHO I AM – 3 out of 50

WHO I AM – 3 out of 50

ALSO BY CORINA STUPU THOMAS

1. **Be a creative explorer** - creative writing, colouring in and collage making workbook for the artist within

2. **We are many people** - colouring book and journal. A perfectly imperfect colouring book and journal for women

3. **108 GRATITUDE JOURNAL** - an ideal tool for the yoga practitioners to deepen their practice

For more information check :
www.beehiveartsstudio.com and
www.etsy.com/shop.beehiverartsstudio
www.corina-stupu-thomas.pixels.com